Table of Contents

Table of Contents

I.   Overview of US Sex Offender Registration

Sex offender registration and notification systems have been established within the United States in a variety of ways. There are a number of resources which are referred to, loosely, as 'sex offender registries.' For the purposes of clarification, we start this summary with an outline of those systems.

Registration is a Local Activity

In the United States, sex offender registration is conducted at the local level. The federal government does not have a comprehensive system for directly registering sex offenders. Generally speaking, sex offenders in the United States[1] are required to register with law enforcement in each state, locality, territory, or tribe within which they reside, work, or attend school.[2]

Each state has its own distinct sex offender registration and notification system. The District of Columbia and the five principal U.S. territories each have their own systems, as well, and an increasing number of federally-recognized Indian Tribes also have their own sex offender registration and notification systems.[3] Every one of these systems has its own nuances and distinct features. Every jurisdiction (meaning each state, territory, or tribe) makes its own determinations about who will be required to register, what information those offenders must provide, which offenders will be posted on the jurisdiction's public registry website, and so forth.

Even though sex offender registration itself is not directly administered by the federal government, the federal government is involved in sex offender registration and notification in a number of meaningful ways.[4]

Federal Minimum Standards

Over the last two decades Congress has enacted various measures setting 'minimum standards' for jurisdictions to implement in their sex offender registration or notification systems. The first of these was passed in 1994 and is commonly referred to as the 'Wetterling Act.' This Act established a set of minimum standards for registration systems for the states.[5] Two years later, in 1996, 'Megan's Law' was passed as a set of minimum standards for community notification.[6] The most recent set of standards can be found in the Sex Offender Registration and Notification Act (SORNA), which was passed in 2006.[7] SORNA currently governs the federal minimum standards for sex offender registration and notification systems.

If a state, tribe, or territory chooses to refrain from substantially implementing SORNA's standards, the jurisdiction risks losing 10 percent of its Edward R. Byrne Justice Assistance Grant (Byrne JAG) funds.[8] As of October 1, 2015, 17 states, 3 territories, and 91 federally-recognized Indian Tribes have substantially implemented SORNA.[9] It is important to note that there are still variations in the registration and notification laws among jurisdictions that have substantially implemented SORNA.[10] Practitioners are advised to become familiar with the specific registration and notification systems in any and all jurisdictions within which they will be working.

National Sex Offender Public Website

The National Sex Offender Public Website (NSOPW), located at www.nsopw.gov, was created by the U.S. Department of Justice in 2005 and is administered by the Office of Sex Offender Sentencing, Monitoring, Apprehending, Registering and Tracking (SMART Office).[11] NSOPW works much like a search engine: jurisdictions that have their own public sex offender registry websites connect to NSOPW by way of a web service or automated upload to enable NSOPW to conduct queries against the jurisdictions' websites. Only information that is publicly disclosed on a jurisdiction's own public sex offender registry website will be displayed in NSOPW's search results, and only the jurisdiction's registry website page will be displayed on the results page of NSOPW. The Department of Justice does not administer any of the registration information that is searched whenever a query is made through NSOPW, and only ensures that the information that is available on jurisdictional websites can be queried through NSOPW.[12]

The National Sex Offender Public Website

www.nsopw.gov

Federal Law Enforcement Databases

Federal databases are utilized by law enforcement across the country to access accurate information about registered sex offenders. Registering agencies and other units of state and local law enforcement submit the information necessary to populate these databases:[13]

1. NSOR: The National Sex Offender Registry (NSOR) is a law-enforcement only database that is a file of the National Crime Information Center (NCIC) database managed by the Federal Bureau of Investigation Criminal Justice Information Services (CJIS) division. It was created in the late 1990s to store data on every registered sex offender in the United States, and to provide access to that data to law enforcement nationwide.[14]

2. NGI: The Next Generation Identification (NGI) system officially replaced the legacy fingerprint database at the FBI (IAFIS) in October of 2014.[15] NGI fingerprint records are linked to the offender's corresponding NSOR record at CJIS; approximately 92% of the records in NSOR have a corresponding fingerprint in NGI.[16]

3. NPPS: The National Palm Print System (NPPS) is the database for palm prints housed with the FBI.

4. CODIS: The Combined DNA Index System (CODIS) is the national DNA database administered by the FBI.

SORNA requires that jurisdictions submit registration information about their registered sex offenders to NSOR, and ensure that offenders' fingerprints have been submitted to NGI, palm prints to NPPS, and DNA profiles to CODIS.[17]

Federal Corrections

Part of the federal government's involvement with sex offenders who are required to register concerns the handling of those offenders as they are housed and subsequently discharged from federal correctional institutions. In particular, concerns have been raised about notifying local law enforcement when a sex offender is released from federal custody. Issues specific to military detention are discussed separately in the section on military registration, below.

1. Bureau of Prisons

BOP does not register sex offenders prior to their release from incarceration, as registration is primarily a state function. However, 18 U.S.C. §4042(c) requires that the Federal Bureau of Prisons (BOP) or a Federal Probation Officer provide notice to the chief law enforcement officer and registration officials of any state, tribe, or local jurisdiction whenever a federal prisoner required to register under SORNA is released from custody.[18] In May of 2014, moreover, BOP issued new guidelines governing its release of prisoners.[19]

2. Bureau of Indian Affairs

The Bureau of Indian Affairs (BIA) operates a number of Detention Centers.[20] However, there are no statutory or administrative requirements for these centers to provide notice to local law enforcement when a sex offender is released from custody. In practice, offenders in BIA facilities generally are not registered prior to their release from incarceration.

3. Immigration and Customs Enforcement

The Department of Homeland Security's (DHS) Immigration and Customs Enforcement (ICE) Enforcement and Removal Operations (ERO) is generally responsible for detaining and deporting undocumented individuals who are present within the United States. As of September 2012, five percent of the nearly 60,000 aliens under an 'Order of Supervision' in the community after being released from detention and pending deportation actions had been previously convicted of a sex offense.[21] ICE-ERO has previously been faulted for having no regular method of notifying local law enforcement when a sex offender, or any offender, is released from ICE-ERO custody.[22] However, in 2015 DHS put forward a rule amending their Privacy Act provisions to permit the transfer of information from DHS to any sex offender registration agency about an offender who is released from DHS custody or removed from the United States.[23] Like the Bureau of Prisons and BIA detention facilities, offenders are not registered prior to their release from ICE custody.

Federal Law Enforcement and Investigations

SORNA designated the United States Marshals Service (USMS) as the lead agency in investigations of suspected violations of the federal law regarding failure to register as a sex offender, which is found at 18 U.S.C. §2250. In order to further their investigative capacity, the USMS has established the National Sex Offender Targeting Center (NSOTC).[24]

Military Registration

If a person resides, works, or attends school on a military base, depending on the source and manner of obtaining the land held by the federal government and housing that base, a state might have no jurisdiction at all over matters occurring thereon. In other words, the base may be a 'federal enclave' where only federal law applies.[25] Because of that, in some locations there may be sex offenders present on military bases who are not required to register with the state because they live, work and attend school solely on land considered to be a federal enclave.

In 2013, Congress enacted a provision that prohibits any person convicted of a felony sex offense from enlisting or being commissioned as an officer in the Armed Forces.[26] In August 2014, the Inspector General of the Department of Defense issued a report regarding DoD's compliance with SORNA.[27] Finally, in March 2015, the Department of Defense issued a directive requiring all installations to identify any affiliated personnel that are required to register as sex offenders, notify state sex offender registries of the presence of those offenders, monitor the offenders while they are on the installation, and report any intended international travel to the U.S. Marshals Service.[28]

Prior to 2015, there had been no provision of federal law (since the passage of SORNA) which enabled or permitted federal authorities to register sex offenders such that the information from those registrations would be connected to any national databases. However, in May 2015, Congress amended SORNA to require the Department of Defense to submit registration information to NSOR and NSOPW on any sex offender who is adjudged by courts-martial or released from a military corrections facility.[29]

Certain components of the Department of Defense have also adopted new policies and procedures to independently track and monitor sex offenders who are either active duty members, civilian employees, contractors, or dependents of active duty members located on U.S. military installations at home and abroad.[30] For example, the Department of the Army now requires all sex offenders who reside or are employed on an Army installation (including those outside of the continental United States) to register with the installation Provost Marshal.[31]

Offenders convicted by military tribunals of registerable sex offenses are required under SORNA to register with any jurisdiction where they live, work or go to school, subject to the limitations described above.[32] Through a series of statutory and administrative cross-references, SORNA requires that persons register as a sex offender whenever they have been convicted of a UCMJ offense listed in Department of Defense Instruction 1325.07, which was revised in 2013.[33]

1. Publication of Sex Assault Courts-Martial Results

The U.S. Marine Corps, Navy, and Air Force have all started to publicly disclose information about convictions for sex offenses, although such disclosures are not occurring on NSOPW at the present time.[34] While it does not make available a universal list of sexual assault Courts-Martial, in 2013, the Army issued a directive to initiate discharge proceedings against any active duty convicted sex offender.[35]

2. Unique Issues for Registration of UCMJ Convictions

Given the unique structure of the military justice system, certain issues arise that are distinct from those in civilian courts. For example, a state-level requirement to register based on a conviction of a sex offense in 'federal court' was held to also include a court-martial from a military court.[36] In at least one state, an offender convicted under article

134 of the UCMJ for an offense relating to child pornography was required to register because the offense of conviction was determined to be a "like violation" to a state offense.[37]

Summary

This hybrid framework of state, territorial, tribal, local, military, and federal laws and policies is the context in which the case law regarding sex offender registration and notification has developed. The summary which follows intentionally avoids any lengthy discussion of the legal issues and case law surrounding prosecutions under 18 U.S.C. §2250, the federal failure to register statute. That topic is worthy of its own guide, and is largely beyond the intended scope of this summary.

II.   Who is Required to Register?

Nearly all registration requirements in the United States are initially triggered by a conviction for a criminal offense.[38] Most jurisdictions limit their registration and notification systems to persons convicted of sex offenses and non-parental kidnapping of a minor. Some states also include other violent or dangerous offenders in their registration and notification system.[39]

'Sex Offenders'

Federal courts have interpreted SORNA as directly imposing a duty on a person to attempt to register if they meet the federal definition of 'sex offender'.[40] SORNA's standards call for jurisdictions to register all persons who have been convicted of a tribal, territory, military, federal, or state sex offense.[41] In addition, certain foreign sex offense convictions will also trigger a registration requirement under SORNA.[42] Generally speaking, however, in practice a jurisdiction will not register an offender unless that jurisdiction's laws require that the offender be registered.[43] However, at least one state has concluded that if a person has ever been required to register as a sex offender pursuant to federal law, that person is required to register in the state.[44] In addition, at least one state will impose the registration requirements of the originating state, even if the new state's requirements are less stringent.[45]

Kidnapping

The inclusion of kidnapping offenses in sex offender registration systems is a legacy of the federal standards discussed above; these offenses have been retained as registerable since the passage of the first federal legislation regarding sex offender registration in 1994. Inclusion of kidnapping offenses in a jurisdiction's sex offender registry has been largely upheld by the courts.[46]

'Catch-All' Provisions

When jurisdictions specifically outline the offenses that require registration, there is little question as to who is required to register. Most jurisdictions, however, also include 'catch-all' provisions which, in varying forms, generally require any person convicted of an offense which is 'by its nature a sex offense' to register as well. One court recently concluded that the state need only prove by 'clear and convincing' evidence that an offender engaged in sexual contact in order to qualify under its catch-all registration provision,[47] while another held that such proof must meet the 'beyond a reasonable doubt' standard.[48]

Comparable Convictions from Other Jurisdictions

A more difficult situation arises when a convicted sex offender moves from one jurisdiction to another, and the new jurisdiction has to make a determination as to whether the person is required to register there. When a person has an out-of-state conviction, most jurisdictions require registration for any offense which is 'comparable,' 'similar,' or 'substantially similar' to one or more of the receiving jurisdiction's registerable offenses.[49] However, when a state's registration system treats persons convicted of in-state offenses differently from those convicted out-of-state, equal protection problems may arise.[50]

Elements vs. Facts

Making the determination as to whether an offense fits under one of these 'catch-all' or 'comparable' provisions has led to a great deal of litigation.[51] Some jurisdictions look at just the elements of the offense of conviction, while others will also look at the facts underlying the conviction.[52] Often, courts take an expansive view of which offenses will trigger registration requirements; though sometimes, the approach can be quite narrow.[53]

Recidivists

In many states, as under SORNA's requirements, an offender who has been convicted of more than one sex offense is subject to heightened registration requirements. One court has held that the two (or more) offenses do not need to arise out of separate proceedings in order to trigger these increased requirements.[54]

III.   Registration of Juvenile Offenders

State juvenile justice systems within the United States have handled juvenile sex offender registration in different ways. For example, at the time of SORNA's passage, 36 states required certain juveniles adjudicated delinquent of sex offenses to register as sex offenders, while the remainder did not require any such juveniles to register. SORNA's minimum standards do require registration for certain juvenile offenders adjudicated delinquent of serious sex offenses.[55] Moreover, SORNA does not require jurisdictions to disclose information about juveniles adjudicated delinquent on their public registry websites.[56]

Juvenile Registration Requirements Vary Across Jurisdictions

Despite SORNA's requirement that juveniles adjudicated delinquent of certain offenses register as a sex offender, the implementation of this provision varies across jurisdictions.[57] Some jurisdictions do not register any juveniles at all; some limit the ages of the offenders who might be registered; some limit the offenses for which they might be registered; and others limit the duration, frequency, or public availability of registration information.[58] Some jurisdictions have mandatory registration provisions for certain juveniles, some are discretionary, and some have a hybrid approach.[59] At least one jurisdiction required a person who committed an offense at age 12 – who would not have been required to register under SORNA had an adjudication occurred at the time of the offense – to register as an adult because the conviction for that offense did not occur until after the individual was 18 years of age.[60]

As with adult registration requirements, registration requirements for juveniles are generally triggered by the equivalent of a conviction for a sex offense in juvenile court, which is typically referred to as an 'adjudication of delinquency.' Most jurisdictions mandate registration for juveniles transferred and convicted for sex offenses in adult court. In addition, one federal circuit court has held that a person previously adjudicated delinquent of a SORNA-registerable offense in state court can be ordered to register as a sex offender as a mandatory condition of probation for a subsequent, unrelated federal conviction.[61]

Because of the varying nature of juvenile justice systems across jurisdictions, problems often arise when a juvenile is adjudicated delinquent in one jurisdiction and then moves to another.[62] Many of those issues mimic the issues discussed above regarding adult offenders.

Issues Unique to Juvenile Adjudications

There are some issues unique to juvenile court cases. When a jurisdiction requires that juveniles subject to registration requirements more onerous than those imposed on adults convicted of the same offense, equal protection issues exist.[63] In two states, the automatic lifetime registration requirement as applied to adjudicated juveniles was held to unconstitutionally violate due process and the prohibition against cruel and unusual punishment.[64] However, when a juvenile court judge refuses to order a juvenile to register, as required by statute, a writ of mandamus may be successfully pursued by the state.[65]

Federal Juvenile Delinquency Act

There are particular issues which arise when a person is ordered to register by a federal court because of a federal adjudication of delinquency for a sex offense.[66] In particular, multiple courts have held that it is not a contravention of the Federal Juvenile Delinquency Act confidentiality provisions to require such individuals to register as a sex offender.[67]

IV.   Retroactive Application & Ex Post Facto Considerations

One of the first issues to be litigated as sex offender registration systems were established across the country was whether or not an offender who had been convicted prior to the passage of the laws requiring registration could be required to register.[68] Numerous challenges to the retroactive application of registration laws were heard throughout the 1990s and 2000s.

United States Supreme Court

In 2003, the United States Supreme Court seemingly settled the issue in the case of Smith v. Doe, a challenge from a sex offender in the State of Alaska who argued that the imposition of registration requirements on him violated the Ex Post Facto clause of the Constitution.[69] The Court held that registration and notification—under the specific facts of that case—were not punitive, and could, therefore, be retroactively imposed as regulatory actions.[70]

While the issue was settled for a time, subsequent litigation has ensued based on increased sex offender registration and notification requirements in many jurisdictions since the Doe decision.[71] In a series of recent cases interpreting 18 U.S.C. §2250, the Supreme Court has declined to take a fresh look at any Ex Post Facto implications raised by the increasing requirements which have been placed on registered sex offenders over the last 12 years.[72]

Significant State Court Decisions

There have been seven state supreme courts in recent years that have held that the retroactive application of their sex offender registration and notification laws violate their respective state constitutions.[73] For example, early in 2015, the New Hampshire Supreme Court held that requiring lifetime registration without the opportunity for review violates the Ex Post Facto provisions of the state's constitution.[74] Similarly, in a recent Pennsylvania case, the retroactive application of a requirement to appear in-person to update any changes to an offender's registration information was held to violate the Ex Post Facto clause.[75] Conversely, however, many state courts continue to stand by the reasoning of the Doe case in continuing to affirm the retroactive application of their own registration laws.[76]

A handful of courts are also requiring the specific performance of a plea agreement or court order when sex offender registration was not actually ordered, was part of the plea negotiations, or given as a specific classification at sentencing.[77] However, on the other hand, this year, California held that a defendant was properly subjected to community notification in 2004 even though he had entered a plea agreement in 1991 which was silent on the issue.[78]

Additional Court Opinions

A review of pertinent federal and state case law reveals that, in one case, a federal court enjoined the enactment of Nevada's SORNA-implementing legislation based on Ex Post Facto concerns,[79] although that injunction has since been lifted.[80] Recently in Texas, a Writ of Mandamus was granted compelling the Department of Public safety to comply with a court order to remove an offender from the registry.[81] In other cases, some offenders have been able to be removed from the registry when the statute is changed in a way which inures to their benefit,[82] but another court has held that increasing the penalties for a failure to register does not violate the Ex Post Facto clause.[83]

Massachusetts recently held that applying community notification retroactively to its existing level two offenders violated due process.[84] Massachusetts also requires a due process hearing before any offender is ordered to comply with its full registration requirements, including those offenders convicted prior to the registration statute's effective date.[85]

V.   Other Constitutional Issues

As previously mentioned, nearly all persons required to register as sex offenders must do so because they have been convicted of a criminal offense. Accordingly, by the time a person is actually required to register, a number of constitutional protections have already been afforded—namely, those which inure to a defendant throughout the course of a criminal trial and sentencing.

Varied Successful Challenges

Although the vast majority of constitutional challenges to sex offender registration and notification requirements have been unsuccessful, there have been some notable decisions based on constitutional grounds. For example, in 2015 a successful challenge was made under the Bill of Attainder clause under article I, section 9 of the U.S. Constitution.[86]

Other examples include opinions issued by state or federal courts which have held that: the collection of internet identifiers violates the First Amendment;[87] being ordered to register as a sex offender triggers the protections of procedural due process;[88] publishing information about an offender's "primary and secondary targets" violates due process;[89] being ordered to register as a parole condition violates due process when the underlying convictions are not sexual in nature;[90] requiring registration for a conviction for solicitation, and not prostitution, when each offense had the same elements, violates due process;[91] a 'three-strikes' sentence based on a failure to register conviction is cruel and unusual punishment;[92] mandatory life imprisonment for a second conviction of failure to register is cruel and unusual punishment;[93] and requiring an offender to continue to register when he had been convicted of having consensual sex with his 14-year old girlfriend (he was 18 at the time) and had his case successfully dismissed under a deferred disposition is cruel and unusual punishment.[94]

Other State Constitutional Provisions

In addition to the decisions above, there have been some notable cases regarding the interaction between SORNA and the existing registration and notification laws in a state: Missouri has held that SORNA preempts state law to the extent that any state constitutional concerns are not implicated;[95] and North Carolina concluded that SORNA is directly incorporated (in part) in to state law and that incorporation is not an unconstitutional delegation of legislative authority.[96] In addition, the Pennsylvania Supreme Court recently invalidated a portion of its sex offender registration law because it violated the 'single subject' rule of the Pennsylvania Constitution.[97]

Jury Determination of Obligation to Register as a Sex Offender

There are a number of cases recently decided by the U.S. Supreme Court which continue to have a bearing on litigation in the field of sex offender registration and notification. For example, the case of Apprendi v. New Jersey has spawned a number of challenges to registration requirements; namely, contending that a jury should be required to determine whether an offender should be subject to the additional 'punishment' of sex offender registration.[98] The test as to whether sex offender registration constitutes 'punishment' is the same as that used to determine whether something is 'punitive' for purposes of an Ex Post Facto analysis as discussed above. To date, most challenges under Apprendi have been unsuccessful.[99]

Ineffective Assistance of Counsel

One frequent argument in failure to register cases is that the offender had ineffective assistance of counsel during the trial for the underlying sex offense, because counsel did not advise them that they would be required to register as a sex offender. Most of these cases have focused on sex offender registration as a 'collateral consequence'[100] of conviction; other cases involving whether a guilty plea is knowing, voluntary and intelligent have also discussed the issue.[101] Recently, though, at least one court has concluded that the heightened registration and notification requirements imposed on sex offenders has rendered any registration requirement a 'direct consequence', rather than a 'collateral consequence', of conviction.[102]

While most courts do not find any constitutional violation in these circumstances, one court held that an affirmative misrepresentation that an offender would not have to register as a sex offender is ineffective assistance of counsel;[103] and another determined that incorrect advice to an offender regarding whether he would be required to register as a sex offender is ineffective assistance of counsel.[104]

Padilla v. Kentucky

Padilla v. Kentucky[105] is a Supreme Court case which held that counsel's failure to correctly advise a client that a conviction would count as a deportable offense under the Immigration and Naturalization Act was deficient assistance under the Sixth Amendment.[106] Since the decision in Padilla, a number of cases have addressed the issue of whether counsel's failure to advise their client that a conviction would result in sex offender registration also runs afoul of the Sixth Amendment.[107] The Supreme Court recently concluded that the holding in Padilla does not apply retroactively.[108]

NFIB v. Sebelius and Arlington v. FCC

While beyond the scope of this update, other recent cases such as National Federation of Independent Business v. Sebelius[109] and Arlington v. FCC[110] are having an impact on certain prosecutions under 18 U.S.C. §2250.[111]

Varied Unsuccessful Challenges

In addition to the challenges described above, offenders often raise other constitutional objections that lead to litigation. In prosecutions for state-level failure to register cases or civil challenges to registration requirements, offenders have launched unsuccessful challenges based on the following arguments: takings,[112] double jeopardy,[113] procedural due process,[114] substantive due process,[115] equal protection,[116] the right to a trial by jury,[117] right to travel,[118] cruel and unusual punishment,[119] full faith & credit,[120] the supremacy clause,[121] and separation of powers.[122] Another set of constitutional arguments are those advanced by the 'sovereign citizen movement' which, though creative, have proven unsuccessful.[123] In addition, in Bond v. U.S.,[124] the Supreme Court granted standing to sex offenders to challenge SORNA on 10th Amendment grounds, where previously they had no standing to do so, but no challenges on those grounds have been successful at the circuit level thus far.[125]

VI.   Community Notification

Every state, tribe and territory that registers sex offenders also makes publicly available certain information about at least some of their sex offenders. While in earlier years community notification was handled via public meetings, fliers, and newspaper announcements, notification has now expanded to include publicly available and searchable websites, which are linked together via NSOPW.

VII.   Failure to Register

For an offender to have any motivation for compliance with the sex offender registration process, there must be an enforcement component. Nearly all jurisdictions which require sex offender registration also have a criminal penalty for failure to register.

The following are a sample of some of the prominent issues which arise in state-level failure to register prosecutions.

Failure to Register as a 'Continuing Offense'

Many jurisdictions hold that a failure to register is a 'continuing offense,' much like larceny or escape, such that a person cannot be prosecuted for multiple failures to register within a given time frame.[126]

Failure to Register as a 'Strict Liability' Offense

Many jurisdictions require a mens rea of some sort to be proven prior to permitting a person to be convicted of failure to register,[127] while others hold that it is a strict liability offense.[128]

Notice

All jurisdictions require that some kind of notice of registration requirements be given to a sex offender prior to their being held criminally liable for a failure to register. That notice can be 'imperfect' and still be sufficient.[129] In other cases, the notice can be constructive, and still valid.[130] However, there are situations where notice will be found insufficient.[131]

Prosecution Based on Failure to Update Information

Most jurisdictions require sex offenders to update their registration information when that registration information changes. In one state, the failure to provide an online identifier supported a conviction for failure to register.[132] In another, however, a change of residence outside of the country did not require the offender to update the state registry.[133]

Venue

Generally speaking, the proper venue for a failure to register case is the jurisdiction in which the person has failed to comply with his registration requirements. In addition, at least one state has held that there is no need to prove where an offender was during the time that he failed to register.[134] The federal failure to register statute, 18 U.S.C. §2250, can also be utilized in cases where there has been interstate travel.

VIII. Residency Restrictions

SORNA's minimum standards do not address or require residency restrictions in any way. One of the most debated collateral consequences of a conviction for a sex offense occurs when a jurisdiction chooses to impose residency restrictions on registered sex offenders, that is, restrictions that prohibit registered sex offenders from residing within a certain perimeter of schools, day care centers, parks, and other locations frequented by children. These residency restrictions are generally passed and enforced on a local or municipal level, although, in some circumstances, a state, tribe, or territory might pass such provisions.[135]

This past year in California, such residency restrictions were held unconstitutional as applied on due process grounds.[136] In New York and some other states, municipal residency restrictions have been invalidated because they were deemed to have been preempted by state law.[137] In another case, the residency restriction was deemed to be punitive and therefore not retroactively applicable.[138] More frequently, however, these locally mandated provisions have been upheld.[139]

IX.   Sex Offender Registration and Notification in Indian Country

As previously discussed, 42 U.S.C. §16927 created, for the first time, a carve-out of state jurisdiction over sex offenders who live, work, or attend school on the lands of certain federally-recognized Indian Tribes. Generally speaking, the tribes that were eligible to opt-in as SORNA registration jurisdictions are those who are not PL-280 tribes. As of September 15, 2015, there are more than 160 federally-recognized tribes operating as SORNA registration jurisdictions; this means that they either have established, or are in the process of establishing, a sex offender registration and notification program.

The vast majority of the 91 tribes that have substantially implemented SORNA, moreover, have utilized the Model Tribal Code, which was developed by Indian Law experts in conjunction with the SMART Office and fully covers all of SORNA's requirements.[140] There are many tribes that have more rigorous registration requirements than the states within which they are located, particularly for those tribes located within states that have not substantially implemented SORNA.[141] For example, in addition to possible criminal sanctions for failure to register, tribes are also generally able to exclude any person (such as a convicted sex offender) from their lands altogether.[142]

There are legal issues unique to Indian Country which impact the registration of tribal sex offenders or the enforcement of sex offender registration requirements against persons who reside on tribal lands or were convicted by tribal courts. For example, because of the different standards regarding the right to counsel in some tribal courts, it is sometimes argued that prosecuting a person based in part on an underlying tribal conviction violates the Sixth Amendment of the U.S. Constitution. Although there are some contrary opinions, and none specifically on point regarding a failure to register prosecution, there is case law to support the argument that convictions for a sex offense in tribal court can form the basis of a federal failure to register conviction.[143]

Tribal Residents and State Registration Responsibilities

Further complications may develop when an offender lives on tribal land but was convicted of a state or federal offense. One question which arises is whether an offender who exclusively lives, works, and attends school on tribal land can be compelled to register with the state within which that tribal land is located. If the offender cannot be compelled to register with the state, it falls to the tribe to register the offender, if the tribe has opted-in to SORNA's provisions and is operating as a registration and notification jurisdiction under its terms.

For example, in New Mexico, the State cannot impose a duty to register on enrolled tribal members living on tribal land who have been convicted of federal sex offenses.[144] At the same time, in neighboring Arizona, persons living in Indian Country are required to keep their registration current with both the state and the tribe.[145] In Arizona, however, a tribal member residing on tribal land cannot be prosecuted under state law for failure to register unless a tribe's registration responsibilities have been delegated to the state via SORNA's delegation procedure.[146]

X.   International Relocation and Registration

In 2011, the SORNA Supplemental Guidelines were issued by the Department of Justice, and added a requirement to SORNA's baseline standards that jurisdictions were required to have their offenders inform them of any intended international travel at least 21 days prior to that travel taking place.[147] Per these standards, offenders are to provide authorities with information regarding their itinerary and intended destinations, among other items, and registration jurisdictions are required to provide this information to the National Sex Offender Targeting Center of the United States Marshals Service.

Prosecution of failure to register cases once a person has left the country has proven difficult on the federal level. While at least one circuit has held that a person can be prosecuted under 18 U.S.C. § 2250 for a failure to update their state registration to reflect that they had departed the country,[148] other circuits have held to the contrary.[149]

To date, more than twenty foreign countries have some form of nationwide or provincial sex offender registration systems. South Korea, the Province of Western Australia, and Canada also make some information publicly available via websites,[150] while other countries have different community notification procedures.[151] The SMART Office also issued the Global Overview of Sex Offender Registration and Notification Systems, which provides more information on international registration and notification systems.[152]

XI.   Miscellaneous

The status of having been convicted of a sex offense, being required to register as a sex offender, or having failed to register as a sex offender, can trigger other legal issues in a variety of contexts.[153] In addition to all of the topics discussed above, the following matters also arise in these circumstances.

Defamation

Defamation is a civil tort action which can be pursued when someone's reputation in the community has been injured by false or malicious statements.[154] Some individuals have unsuccessfully made claims under 42 U.S.C. § 1983 on the basis of defamation, when they were posted on the sex offender registry website without the due process provided by statute.[155]

Deportation

Convictions for a failure to register have triggered subsequent deportation proceedings in some cases. There is a circuit split as to whether a conviction for a state failure to register offense is a crime involving 'moral turpitude' under the immigration code such that a person is removable because of that conviction.[156]

Fair Credit Reporting Act

Certain people have had limited success in pursuing claims under the Fair Credit Reporting Act (FCRA) when they have been incorrectly reported by a credit bureau as having prior sex offense convictions.[157]

Homeless & Transient Offenders

Homeless or transient sex offenders have generated a great deal of litigation as states have tried to enforce registration requirements. Many states are rewriting their laws in such a way that these offenders are clearly required to register.[158] This issue has recently come to the fore in the City of Chicago, where there has been a great deal of civil litigation based on its policy to deny registration to any sex offender who lacked a fixed address.[159]

In most cases, an offender's homelessness has not prevented a successful prosecution for failure to register, although sometimes statutory or evidentiary problems have prevented successful prosecution.[160] Differing check-in requirements for homeless offenders as opposed to offenders who have a residence address have been affirmed.[161] In one case, a court found that when an offender repeatedly uses a 'mail drop' address as his legal address, he 'resides' at that location for the purposes of a prosecution for failure to register as a sex offender.[162] In another, when an offender still technically lived at the same address, even though he lived in an outbuilding or his truck rather than the main residence, he could not be prosecuted for a failure to update his residence address.[163] However, in an attempt to prosecute a long-haul trucker for failure to register, a conviction could not be had, even when he had prolonged absences from his registered residence.[164]

HUD Housing

One collateral consequence of a state-imposed lifetime sex offender registration requirement is that a person is no longer permitted, pursuant to federal law, to be admitted to any "federally assisted housing."[165] However, once a person has been admitted to a program such as Section 8,[166] they cannot be thereafter terminated because of a new, or newly-discovered, lifetime sex offender registration requirement.[167] A person may be prosecuted for perjury if they have lied on an application for Section 8 housing about the status of a lifetime registered sex offender living in the residence.[168] One recent case permitted the termination of a beneficiary's assistance based only on the address displayed on the public sex offender registry website for a jurisdiction.[169]

Impeachment

Generally speaking, rules of evidence permit attacking the credibility of a witness by way of introducing evidence of certain prior convictions. In one state, a conviction for failure to register was determined to be a 'crime of deception', rendering it admissible in a subsequent criminal trial to impeach the defendant's testimony.[170]

Sentencing Enhancement Under Federal Law

Under federal law, additional punishment can result if certain crimes are committed while an offender is required to register as a sex offender. Under 18 U.S.C. §2260A, the commission of certain offenses against a minor while the perpetrator is required to register as a sex offender under any law will result in a ten year mandatory minimum sentence to run consecutively to any other sentences imposed.[171] The retroactive application of these provisions does not violate the Ex Post Facto clause.[172]

XII.   Conclusion

The statutes, regulations and laws addressing sex offender registration and notification in the United States are varied and complex. While this summary seeks to provide updated and accurate information, practitioners are advised to conduct their own research to confirm that they are utilizing the most current information available and applicable in their jurisdiction.

For any questions about SORNA itself or for more information about any of the SMART Office projects described in this resource, please feel free to contact the SMART Office at asksmart@usdoj.gov or visit our website at www.smart.gov.

---

[1]   Except for military offenders, addressed in more detail below, in section I.

[2]   Colleges must also annually include in a security report a statement advising the campus community the location where information about registered sex offenders on campus may be obtained. Violence Against Women Act; Final Rule, 79 Fed. Reg. 62,785-86 (Oct. 20, 2014).

[3]   Federally-recognized Indian Tribes located in 'PL-280' states will typically have their registration functions handled by the state within which their lands are located. 42 U.S.C. § 16927(a)(2)(A), citing Pub. L. No. 83-280, c. 505, 67 Stat. 588 (1953) (codified at 18 U.S.C. § 1162).

[4]   CONG. RESEARCH SERVICE REPORT 7-5700, FEDERAL INVOLVEMENT IN SEX OFFENDER REGISTRATION AND NOTIFICATION: OVERVIEW AND ISSUES FOR CONGRESS, IN BRIEF (March 25, 2015), https://www.fas.org/sgp/crs/misc/R43954.pdf.

[5]   Jacob Wetterling Crimes Against Children and Sexually Violent Offender Registration Act, Pub. L. No. 103-322, § 170101, 108 Stat. 2038 (1994). This was an incentive-based system, where States would be penalized (via loss of federal grant funds) for a failure to implement its terms. The five principal U.S. territories (American Samoa, Commonwealth of the Northern Mariana Islands, Guam, Puerto Rico, and the U.S. Virgin Islands) were included under Wetterling's requirements by way of Final Guidelines issued in April of 1996. Final Guidelines for the Jacob Wetterling Crimes Against Children and Sexually Violent Offender Registration Act, 61 Fed. Reg. 15,110 (April 4, 1996).

[6]   In the same way that the Wetterling Act's provisions were incentive-based (see supra text accompanying note 5), so were the provisions of Megan's Law.

[7]   42 U.S.C. §§ 16901-16946. All United States Code references are current as of July 2015. Two sets of guidelines have been issued to assist in the implementation of SORNA. The National Guidelines for Sex Offender Registration and Notification, 73 Fed. Reg. 38,030 (July 2, 2008) [hereinafter Final Guidelines], Supplemental Guidelines for Sex Offender Registration and Notification, 76 Fed. Reg. 1630 (Jan. 11, 2011) [hereinafter Supplemental Guidelines]. Guidelines provisions, standing alone, do not create an additional basis for criminal liability under 18 U.S.C. §2250, United States v. Belaire, 480 Fed. Appx. 284 (5th Cir. 2012) (defendant could not be prosecuted for failing to update 'temporary lodging'ation when neither originating nor destination state required such information to be provided); but see United States v. Piper, 2013 U.S. Dist. LEXIS 113059 (D. Vt. Aug. 12, 2013).

[8]   For any State or Territory, the penalty is contained in 42 U.S.C. § 16925:

> For any fiscal year after the end of the period for implementation, a jurisdiction that fails, as determined by the Attorney General, to substantially implement this title shall not receive 10 percent of the funds that would otherwise be allocated for that fiscal year to the jurisdiction under subpart 1 of part E of title I of the Omnibus Crime Control and Safe Streets Act of 1968 (42 U.S.C. § 3750, et seq.).

If the 10 percent penalty is assessed, the jurisdiction can apply for reallocation of those funds to use for purposes of implementing SORNA.

For Tribes that elected to function as registration jurisdictions, the penalty contained in 42 U.S.C. § 16925 may apply, if the tribe qualifies for that funding, which is determined by formula. However, there is a separate and significant penalty for non-compliance by tribes contained in 42 U.S.C. § 16927: For any federally-recognized Indian Tribe that the Attorney General determines has "not substantially implemented the requirements of [SORNA] and is not likely to become capable of doing so within a reasonable amount of time," the statute creates automatic delegation of SORNA functions:

> . . . to another jurisdiction or jurisdictions within which the territory of the tribe is located [and requires the tribe] to provide access to its territory and such other cooperation and assistance as may be needed to enable such other jurisdiction or jurisdictions to carry out and enforce the requirements of [SORNA].

The meaning of "provide access" and other issues regarding delegation of registration and notification responsibilities under SORNA for federally-recognized Indian Tribes is discussed in documents #12 and #13 of the SMART Office's "Topics in SORNA Implementation" series, available at http://www.smart.gov/pdfs/SORNA_ImplementationDocuments.pdf.

[9]   Current as of October 1, 2015. For the current list of implemented jurisdictions, please visit http://www.smart.gov/newsroom_jurisdictions_sorna.htm. For a comprehensive report on the efforts and challenges in implementing SORNA, see GAO-13-211, SEX OFFENDER REGISTRATION AND NOTIFICATION ACT: JURISDICTIONS FACE CHALLENGES TO IMPLEMENTING THE ACT, AND STAKEHOLDERS REPORT POSITIVE AND NEGATIVE EFFECTS (2013), available at http://www.gao.gov/assets/660/652032.pdf.

[10] Official reports detailing the systems of each jurisdiction which has substantially implemented SORNA are available on the SMART Office web site at http://www.smart.gov/sorna.htm.

[11] The precursor of NSOPW was NSOPR, the National Sex Offender Public Registry, which was the official name of the website from the time of its administrative creation in 2005 until the passage of SORNA in 2006. Press Release, Dep't of Justice, Office of Justice Programs, Department of Justice Activates National Sex Offender Public Registry Website (July 20, 2005), available at http://www.amberalert.gov/newsroom/pressreleases/ojp_05_0720.htm. By July of 2006, all fifty states were linked to NSOPR. Press Release, Dep't of Justice, Office of Justice Programs, All 50 States Linked to Department of Justice National Sex Offender Public Registry Website (July 3, 2006), available at http://www.justice.gov/opa/pr/2006/July/06_ag_414 html.

[12] The SMART Office administers the Tribe and Territory Sex Offender Registry System (TTSORS), which is a system developed particularly for federally-recognized Indian Tribes and U.S. Territories which had not previously operated a sex offender registration system or website. All of the information in TTSORS is supplied and administered by the jurisdictions. More information about TTSORS is available at http://www.smart.gov/pdfs/TTSORSFactSheet.pdf.

[13] For example, a local police department might submit an offender's fingerprints to the FBI at the time of arrest.

[14] See Pam Lychner Sexual Offender Tracking and Identification Act of 1996, Pub. L. No. 104-236, 110 Stat. 3093.

[15] NGI Officially Replaces IAFIS—Yields More Search Options and Investigative Leads, and Increased Identification Accuracy, https://www.fbi.gov/about-us/cjis/cjis-link/october%202014/ngi- officially-replaces-iafisyields-more-search-options-and-investigative-leads-and-increased-identification-accuracy.

[16] Conversation with Zachary Hartzell, FBI CJIS Division, NCIC Operations and Policy Unit, 2010.

[17] In many cases, an offender will have had their fingerprints, palm prints or DNA submitted prior to the registration process, as part of their arrest, sentencing, incarceration, or at some other point in the processing of their case. Registration agencies are not required to submit duplicate entries to federal databases where a fingerprint, palm print, or DNA record already exists. Final Guidelines, supra note 7, at 38,057.

[18] 18 U.S.C. § 4042(c). The Bureau of Prisons is a Department of Justice subdivision and part of the Executive Branch. Federal probation officers are governed by the Administrative Office of the United States Courts, a Judicial Branch Office.

[19] Program Statement 5110.15, Notification Requirements Upon Release of Sex Offenders, Violent Offenders, and Drug Traffickers (May 16, 2014), available at http://www.bop.gov/policy/progstat/5110_017.pdf. The form utilized by BOP to provide notice of registration responsibilities to its prisoners upon release can be found at http://www.bop.gov/policy/forms/BP_A0648.pdf.

[20] BIA is part of the Department of the Interior, in the Executive Branch. See generally Office of the Inspector General Report #WR-EV-BIA-0005-2010, BUREAU OF INDIAN AFFAIRS' DETENTION FACILITIES (March 2011) ("BIA reported that as of September 2009, the detention program consisted of 94 detention facilities: 23 bureau-operated facilities, 52 tribally-operated facilities under Public Law (P.L.) 93-638 contracts, and 19 tribally-operated facilities under self-governance compact agreements"), available at http://www.doi.gov/oig/reports/upload/01-WR-EV-BIA-0005-2010Public.pdf.

[21] GAO-13-832, ICE COULD BETTER INFORM OFFENDERS IT SUPERVISES OF REGISTRATION RESPONSIBILITIES AND NOTIFY JURISDICTIONS WHEN OFFENDERS ARE REMOVED (2013) at p. 1, available at http://www.gao.gov/assets/660/657831.pdf.

[22] See id.

[23] Notice of Amendment of Privacy Act System of Records, 80 Fed. Reg. 24,269 § HH (April 30, 2015). ICE-ERO is now using the SORNA Exchange Portal to provide notifications to jurisdictions when a sex offender is released from ICE-ERO custody. For additional information about the SORNA Exchange Portal, see http://www.smart.gov/pdfs/SORNA_Portalfactsheet.pdf.

[24] The National Center for Missing and Exploited Children (NCMEC) operates the Sex Offender Tracking Team (SOTT) which is collocated with NSOTC in Crystal City, Virginia. SOTT publishes a bi-

annual survey of the number of registered sex offenders in the United States. http://www.missingkids.com/ en_US/documents/Sex_Offenders_Map.pdf. As of June 1, 2015, there were 843,260 registered sex offenders in the United States. For more information about SOTT, see http://www.missingkids.com/SOTT.

[25]   'Federal Enclave' is a legal term of art which refers to property that is either in whole or in part under the law enforcement jurisdiction of the United States Government. See generally the 'Enclave Clause,' U.S. CONST. art. I, § 8, cl. 17 ("[The Congress shall have Power...] [t]o exercise exclusive Legislation in all Cases whatsoever, over such District (not exceeding ten miles square) as may, by Cession of particular States, and the Acceptance of Congress, become the Seat of the Government of the United States, and to exercise like Authority over all Places purchased by the Consent of the Legislature of the State in which the Same shall be, for the Erection of Forts, Magazines, Arsenals, dock-Yards, and other needful Buildings"); see also 40 U.S.C. § 3112 (2006) (concerning federal jurisdiction). A similar issue arises regarding offenders located within National Parks or other federally-held land that holds the status of 'federal enclave.'

[26]   National Defense Authorization Act for Fiscal Year 2013, Pub. L. No. 112-239, § 523, 126 Stat. 1632, 1636 (codified at 10 U.S.C. § 504 note). This general prohibition also extends to federal convictions, juvenile adjudications, and situations where the disposition of the case requires the person to register as a sex offender, regardless of the offense of conviction. Enlistment, Appointment, and Induction Criteria, 32 C.F.R. § 66.6(b)(8)(iii) (2015).

[27]   DODIG-2014-103, Evaluation of DoD Compliance with the Sex Offender Registration and Notification Act (August 29, 2014), http://www.dodig.mil/pubs/documents/DODIG-2014-103.pdf.

[28]   Registered Sex Offender (RSO) Identification, Notification, and Monitoring in DoD, Directive-Type Memorandum (DTM) 15-003 (March 26, 2015), http://www.dtic mil/whs/directives/corres/pdf/DTM15003.pdf.

[29]   Military Sex Offender Reporting Act of 2015 (Title V of the Justice for Victims of Trafficking Act of 2015), Pub. L. No. 114-22, § 502, 129 Stat. 227 (codified at 42 U.S.C. § 16928a).

[30]   See Army Regulation 190-45, § 2-7 (2007).

[31]   Registration of Sex Offenders on Army Installations (inside and outside the Continental United States), 32 C.F.R. § 635.6 (2015). Provost Marshal officials have also been directed to seek to establish Memoranda of Understanding with state and local sex offender registration officials to facilitate the flow of information regarding sex offenders (along with other criminal justice information). Establishing Memoranda of Understanding, 32 C.F.R. § 635.20 (2015).

[32]   U.S. v. Kebodeaux, 133 S.Ct. 2496 (2013).

[33]   Administration of Military Correctional Facilities and Clemency and Parole Authority, Dep't of Defense Instruction 1325.07, Appx. 4 to Enc. 2 (March 11, 2013), http://www.dtic mil/whs/directives/ corres/pdf/132507p.pdf. Although the United States Coast Guard is technically a part of the Department of Homeland Security, this Instruction (along with the DTM referenced supra n. 28) also governs their proceedings. See Kebodeaux, 133 S.Ct. at 2496.

[34]   Navy courts-martial results are available every month, and the most recent report can be found at http://www navy.mil/submit/display.asp?story_id=91604 (September 2015). USMC courts-martial summaries are available by region and can be viewed at
http://www mciwest.marines mil/StaffOffices/LegalServicesSupportSectionWest/CourtMartialResults.aspx and http://www.mcieast.marines mil/StaffOffices/LegalServicesSupportSectionEast/ EasternRegionalTrialCoun selOffice/CourtsMartialResults.aspx (courts-martial page does not appear to be populated at the time of publication); a summary version is very difficult to find, the most recent document being
http://www hqmc.marines.mil/portals/61/Docs/courtsmartial0514.pdf. A four-year summary of Air Force Courts-Martial for sexual assault can be found at http://www.afjag.af.mil/shared/media/document/AFD-130917-06htpdfeto Rico, Army to Discharge Convicted Sex Offenders, MILITARY TIMES (Nov. 20, 2013), http://www militarytimes.com/article/20131120/NEWS/311200024/Army-discharge-convicted-sex- offenders.

[36]   Billingsley v. Alabama, 2012 Ala. Crim. App. LEXIS 112 (Ala. Crim. App. 2012).

[37]   Doe v. Sex Offender Registry Board, 23 N.E.3d 938 (Mass. 2015).

[38]   Withheld adjudications have been held to require registration under SORNA. See U.S. v. Bridges, 901 F. Supp. 2d 677 (W.D. Va. 2012), aff'd, 741 F.3d 464 (4th Cir. 2014) (withheld adjudication in Florida registerable under SORNA); Roe v. Replogle, 408 S.W.3d 759 (Mo. 2013) ("suspended imposition of sentence" is a 'conviction' under SORNA). In some jurisdictions, registration is required when a person has been civilly committed, received a withheld adjudication, found 'Not Guilty by Reason of Insanity' or incompetent to stand trial, or when ordered to register by a probation officer. See Mayo v. People, 181 P.3d 1207 (Colo. App. 2008) (civil commitment triggered requirement to register); Price v. State, 43 So.3d 854 (Fla. Dist. Ct. App. 2010) (withheld adjudication); State v. Cardona, 986 N.E.2d 66 (Ill. 2013) (a finding of 'not not guilty' for an incompetent defendant sufficient to require registration); State v. Olsson, 958 N.E.2d 356 (Ill. App. Ct. 2011) (defendant found incompetent to stand trial was required to register); In re Kasckarow, 936 N.Y.S.2d 498 (N.Y. Sup. Ct. 2013) (nolo contendere plea and withheld adjudication in Florida registerable in New York); Walters v. Cooper, 739 S.E.2d 185 (N.C. Ct. App.), aff'd, 748 S.E.2d 144 (N.C. 2013) ('Prayer for Judgment Continued' on a charge of sexual battery is a final conviction triggering requirement to register). But see United States v. Moore, 449 Fed. Appx. 677 (9th Cir. 2011) (probation condition under SORNA requiring registration for a tier I offender more than 15 years after the conviction was invalid). In addition, some jurisdictions require registration even if an offender has been pardoned of the underlying offense, In re Edwards, 720 S.E.2d 462 (S.C. 2011), had their underlying complaint dismissed and pleas vacated under a special statutory procedure, People v. Hamdon, 225 Cal. App. 4th 1065 (2014) (procedure under California Penal Code 1203.4a), Witten v. State, 2014 Miss. LEXIS 308 (June 26, 2014) (procedure under California Penal Code 1203.4a), had their conviction for a sex offense vacated on double jeopardy grounds, Montoya v. Driggers, 320 P.3d 987 (N.M. 2014), and in some jurisdictions an offender can remain on the public registry website even if that offender no longer has any meaningful ties to the jurisdiction, Doe v. O'Donnell, 924 N.Y.S.2d 684 (N.Y. App. Div. 2011). But see Stallworth v. Mississippi, 160 So.3d 1161 (Miss. 2015) (expungement of underlying conviction from Maryland entitles the defendant to relief from registration responsibilities in Mississippi).

[39] For example, Montana's Violent Offender registry (http://svcalt.mt.gov/svor/search.asp) is displayed together with its sex offender registry information. See Mont. Code § 46-23-502(13) (definition of 'violent offense'). Other states have registries for other kinds of offenses. See State v. Brown, 301 P.3d 789 (Kan. Ct. App. 2013) (describing Kansas' drug offense registry); http://www.news-journal.com/news/2014/Officials-target-abuse-recidivism (Texas establishes domestic violence registry); Ben Winslow, Governor Signs More Bills into Law, Including 'White Collar Crime Registry', Fox 13 Now (March 24, 2015), available at http://fox13now.com/2015/03/24/governor-signs-more-bills- into-law-including-white-collar-crime-registry/ (Utah).

[40]   42 U.S.C. § 16911(1). The bulk of these cases have been appeals of convictions under 18 U.S.C. § 2250 and interpret the "initial registration" requirement contained in 42 U.S.C. § 16913. See Carr v. United States, 560 U.S. 438 (2010).

[41]   "Sex Offense" is defined in 42 U.S.C. § 16911(5)(A). For guidance on which persons convicted of UCMJ offenses are required to register, see United States v. Jones, 383 Fed. Appx. 885 (11th Cir. 2010) and Dep't of Defense Instruction 1325.07, supra n. 33.

[42]   42 U.S.C. § 16911(5)(B). See McCarty v. Roos, 2014 U.S. Dist. LEXIS 48363 (D. Nev., Apr. 8 2014) (describing the standard for registering a Japanese conviction under SORNA).

[43]   In other words, there will be situations where SORNA imposes a registration requirement directly on an offender, but the jurisdiction where that offender lives, works or attends school refuses to register him, because the jurisdiction's laws do not require registration for the offense of conviction. See Dep't of Pub. Safety v. Doe, 94 A.3d 791 (Md. 2014) (State is not required to register an offender if the state's laws do not require it).

[44]   Doe v. Toelke, 389 S.W.3d 165 (Mo. 2012) ("the [state] registration requirements apply to any person who 'has been' required to register as a sex offender pursuant to federal law. Consequently, even if Doe presently is not required to register pursuant to SORNA, he 'has been' required to register as a sex offender and, therefore, is required to register [with the state].") (offender convicted in 1983 required to

register, even though Missouri law only requires registration of persons convicted on or after January 1, 1995).

[45]   Oulman v. Setter, 2014 Minn. App. Unpub. LEXIS 842 (Aug. 4, 2014) (Colorado registration requirements imposed on offender who relocated to Minnesota).

[46]   See Rainer v. State, 690 S.E.2d 827 (Ga. 2010) (non-parental false imprisonment is registerable), Moffitt v. Commonwealth, 360 S.W.3d 247 (Ky. Ct. App. 2012) (citing the legislative history of the Wetterling Act to support registration for kidnapping); People v. Knox, 903 N.E.2d 1149 (N.Y. 2009) (non-parental kidnapping and unlawful imprisonment is registerable); State v. Smith, 780 N.W.2d 90 (Wisc. 2010) (non-parental false imprisonment is registerable).

[47]   State v. Norman, 824 N.W.2d 739 (Neb. 2013).

[48]   In re K.B., 285 P.3d 389 (Kan. Ct. App. 2012).

[49]   See Doe v. Board, 925 N.E.2d 533 (Mass. 2010) (Maine conviction for unlawful sexual contact registerable in Massachusetts); Skaggs v. Neb. State Patrol, 804 N.W.2d 611 (Neb. 2011) (California conviction registerable in Nebraska); Lozada v. South Carolina Law Enforcement Division, 719 S.E.2d 258 (S.C. 2011) (Pennsylvania conviction for unlawful restraint registerable as kidnapping in South Carolina); In re Shaquille O'Neal B., 684 S.E.2d 549 (S.C. 2009) (North Carolina juvenile adjudication for 'indecent liberties between children' registerable in South Carolina); State v. Harbin, 2014 Tenn. Crim. App. LEXIS 959 (Oct. 15. 2014) (Michigan conviction for criminal sexual conduct registerable in Tennessee); Scott v. State, 2014 Tex. App. LEXIS 11410 (Oct. 16, 2014) (Illinois conviction for criminal sexual assault registerable in Texas). But see People v. Brooks, 296 P.3d 216 (Co. 2012) (Texas conviction not registerable in Colorado); Sharma v. State, 670 S.E.2d 494 (Ga. Ct. App. 2008) (Texas conviction not registerable in Georgia); State v. Frederick, 251 P.3d 48 (Kan. 2011) (Minnesota adjudication for criminal sexual conduct not registerable in Kansas because it is not a 'conviction' under Kansas law); Doe v. Sex Offender Registry Board, 11 N.E.3d 153 (Mass. App. Ct. 2014) (Federal conviction for Kidnapping of a minor not registerable in Massachusetts), State v. Orr, 304 P.3d 449 (N.M. Ct. App. 2013) (conviction for 'taking indecent liberties with children' in North Carolina not registerable in New Mexico); State v. Hall, 294 P.3d 1235 (N.M. 2013) (California conviction for 'annoying or molesting children' not registerable in New Mexico without evidence of actual conduct comparable to New Mexico offense, regardless of the elements of the offense); Dep't Pub. Safety v. Anonymous, 382 S.W.3d 531 (Tex. App. 2012) (Massachusetts conviction for indecent assault and battery not registerable in Texas); Ex parte Harbin, 297 S.W.3d 283 (Tex. Crim. App. 2009) (California conviction for 'annoying or molesting a child' not registerable in Texas); State v. Howe, 212 P.3d 565 (Wash. 2009) (California conviction for 'lewd acts upon a child' not registerable in Washington); State v. Werneth, 197 P.3d 1195 (Wash. Ct. App. 2008) (Georgia conviction for child molestation not registerable in Washington State).

[50]   See Doe v. Pa. Bd. of Prob. & Parole, 513 F.3d 95 (3d Cir. 2008) (Pennsylvania's disparate treatment of in-state and out-of-state offenders violated the Equal Protection Clause of the 14th Amendment).

[51]   See United States v. Dodge, 597 F.3d 1347 (11th Cir. 2010) (18 USC § 1470 registerable under SORNA, even though it is not listed); United States v. Hahn, 551 F. 3d 977 (10th Cir. 2008) (probation conditions properly required registration in a fraud case when there was a prior state conviction for a sex offense); United States v. Byun, 539 F.3d 982 (9th Cir. 2008) (conviction for alien smuggling which had underlying facts of sex trafficking properly triggered registration); United States v. Jensen, 278 Fed. Appx. 548 (6th Cir. 2008) (Conspiracy to Commit Sexual Abuse is a registerable offense). But see United States v. Jimenez, 275 Fed. Appx. 433 (5th Cir. 2008) (where only evidence of sexual misconduct was three unsubstantiated police reports, registration requirement was inappropriate); State v. Coman, 273 P.3d 701 (Kan. 2012) (bestiality is not a registerable offense); State v. Haynes, 760 N.W.2d 283 (Mich. App. 2008) (bestiality not registerable).

[52]   See, e.g., Commonwealth v. Sampolski, 89 A.3d 1287 (Pa. Super. Ct. 2014) (looking to the elements of the offense), Doe v. Sex Offender Registry Bd., 925 N.E.2d 533 (Mass. 2010) (may not consider facts underlying the conviction).

[53]   See, e.g., State v. Duran, 967 A.2d 184 (Md. 2009) (determining that Indecent Exposure was not registerable because the lewdness element of the crime incorporated conduct that was not sexual in addition to that which could be sexual).

[54]   Ward v. State, 288 P.3d 94 (Alaska 2012). SORNA's provisions for enhanced tiering of recidivists are found in 42 U.S.C. § 16911(3)(C) & § 16911(4)(C).

[55]   SORNA's minimum standards require that jurisdictions register juveniles who were at least 14 years old at the time of the offense and who have been adjudicated delinquent for committing (or attempting or conspiring to commit) a sexual act with another by force, by the threat of serious violence, or by rendering unconscious or drugging the victim. "Sexual Act" is defined in 18 U.S.C. § 2246.

[56]   The Supplemental Guidelines give jurisdictions full discretion over whether they will post information about juveniles adjudicated delinquent of sex offenses on their public registry website. Supplemental Guidelines, supra note 7 at 1636-37.

[57]   A survey of the varying juvenile registration responsibilities imposed by each state can be found in A Snapshot of Juvenile Registration and Notification Laws: A Survey of the United States (2011), http://www njjn.org/uploads/digital-library/SNAPSHOT_web10-28.pdf.

[58]   See, e.g., Clark v. State, 957 A.2d 1 (Del. 2008) (lifetime registration requirement for juvenile was not contravened by requirement to consider the 'best interests of the child' in fashioning a disposition). Some states go beyond SORNA's requirements. See, e.g., State v. I.C.S., 145 So.3d 350 (La. 2014) (defendants who committed sex offenses prior to age 14, were not transferrable to adult court at that age, and whose offenses did not require registration upon a juvenile adjudication of delinquency, were prosecuted in adult court in their twenties for those offenses and required to register); In re J.L., 800 N.W.2d 720 (S.D. 2011) (14 year-old boy adjudicated delinquent for consensual sex with his 12 year-old girlfriend was ordered to register for life).

[59]   See, e.g., N.V. v. State, 2008 Ark. App. LEXIS 207 (March 5, 2008) (due process hearing required prior to juvenile being required to register); N.L. v. State, 989 N.E.2d 773 (Ind. 2013) (adjudicated juvenile may only be required to register after an evidentiary hearing, using the 'clear and convincing' standard). For a complete summary of the juvenile registration schemes across the United States, see SMART SUMMARY: PROSECUTION, TRANSFER, AND REGISTRATION OF SERIOUS JUVENILE SEX OFFENDERS, http://www.smart.gov/pdfs/SMARTSummary.pdf   (2015).

[60]   State v. I.C.S., supra n. 58.

[61]   U.S. v. Shannon, 511 Fed. Appx. 487 (6th Cir. 2013) (Ohio adjudication for Gross Sexual Imposition triggered registration condition in subsequent sentencing for possession of a firearm by a felon).

[62]   See, e.g., In re Crockett, 159 Cal. App. 4th 751 (Cal. Ct. App. 2008) (juvenile adjudicated delinquent of sex offense in Texas was not required to register when he moved to California); Murphy v. Commonwealth, 2015 Ky. App. Unpub. LEXIS 275 (Apr. 24, 2015) (juvenile adjudicated delinquent in Michigan required to register in Kentucky, even though Kentucky-adjudicated juveniles are not required to register); Smith v. Commonwealth, 2014 Ky. App. Unpub. LEXIS 728 (Sept. 12, 2014) (Illinois- adjudicated offender required to register in Kentucky because he was required to register in Illinois). Nebraska also only requires registration for a juvenile adjudication of delinquency for a sex offense when the offender is convicted outside of Nebraska and has a registration requirement imposed by another state. See Nebraska Sex Offender Registry: FAQ's, https://sor nebraska.gov/FAQ (last visited July 13, 2015); see also A.W. v. Nebraska, 2015 U.S. Dist. LEXIS 48287 (D. Neb. April 13, 2015) (refusing to certify the question of the constitutionality of requiring an out-of-state adjudicated juvenile to be subject to public notification in Nebraska to the Nebraska Supreme Court).

[63]   See In re Z.B., 757 N.W.2d 595 (S.D. 2008) (treating juvenile sex offenders convicted of the same crimes as adult sex offenders differently and more harshly than the adult sex offenders served no rational purpose and violated the Equal Protection Clause of the 14th Amendment); cf. In re C.P.T., 2008 Minn. App. Unpub. LEXIS 929 (Aug. 5, 2008) (lifetime registration requirement for juveniles does not violate due process).

[64]   In re C.P., 967 N.E.2d 729 (Ohio 2012) (due process and the prohibition against cruel and unusual punishment); In re J.B., 107 A.3d 1 (Pa. 2014) (procedural due process). Other courts have held that registration requirements as applied to juveniles adjudicated delinquent of a sex offense does not violate the 8th Amendment. United States v. Under Seal, 709 F.3d 257 (4th Cir. 2013) (military conviction); see also In re Justin B., 747 S.E.2d 774 (S.C. 2013) (lifetime GPS monitoring of a juvenile adjudicated delinquent of a sex offense does not violate the 8th Amendment).

[65]   Illinois ex. rel. Birkett v. Konetski, 909 N.E.2d 783 (Ill. 2009).

[66]   In 2010 the U.S. Supreme Court granted certiorari in a case where the Ninth Circuit had held that the juvenile registration provisions of SORNA were unconstitutional when applied retroactively. U.S. v. Juvenile Male, 581 F.3d 977 (2009), vacated and remanded, 131 S. Ct. 2860 (2011), appeal dismissed as moot, 653 F.3d 1081 (9th Cir. 2011). In its decision, however, the Supreme Court did not in any way address the question of the constitutionality of the retroactive application of SORNA's requirement that certain adjudicated juveniles register as sex offenders.

[67]   U.S. v. Under Seal, 709 F.3d 257 (4th Cir. 2013) (military conviction); United States v. Juvenile Male, 670 F.3d 999 (9th Cir. 2012). The Federal Juvenile Delinquency Act is found at 18 U.S.C. §5031, et. seq.

[68]   SORNA requires that jurisdictions register offenders whose "predicate convictions predate the enactment of SORNA or the implementation of SORNA in the jurisdiction" when an offender is:

    (1) incarcerated or under supervision, either for the predicate sex offense or for some other crime;

    (2) already registered or subject to a pre-existing sex offender registration requirement under the jurisdiction's law; or

    (3) reenter the jurisdiction's justice system because of a subsequent felony conviction.

Final Guidelines, supra n. 7, at 38046; Supplemental Guidelines, supra n. 7, at 1639.

[69]   Smith v. Doe, 538 U.S. 1009 (2003).

[70]   Id.

[71]   See, e.g., Jensen v. State, 905 N.E.2d 384 (Ind. 2009) (person convicted after the initial passage of the law could be required to comply with amended requirements).

[72]   See U.S. v. Kebodeaux, 133 S.Ct. 2496 (2013) (assuming without deciding that Congress did not violate the Ex Post Facto clause in enacting SORNA's registration requirements); U.S. v. Juvenile Male, 131 S.Ct. 2860 (2011) (declining to address whether SORNA's requirements violated the Ex Post Facto clause on grounds of mootness); Carr v. U.S., 560 U.S. 438 (2010) (declining to address the issue of whether SORNA violates the Ex Post Facto clause).

[73]   Doe v. State, 189 P.3d 999 (Alaska 2008); Wallace v. State, 905 N.E.2d 371 (Ind. 2009); Maine v. Letalien, 985 A.2d 4 (Me. 2009); Doe v. Dep't of Pub. Safety & Corr. Servs., 40 A.3d 39 (Md. 2013); State v. Williams, 952 N.E.2d 1108 (Ohio 2011); Starkey v. Okla. Dep't of Corr., 305 P.3d 1004 (Okla. 2013) (detailing all case law from state courts regarding retroactive application of sex offender registration and notification statutes). One additional case along these lines, Doe v. Phillips, 194 S.W.3d 833 (Mo. 2006), has subsequently been rendered moot, Doe v. Keathley, 2009 Mo. App. LEXIS 4 (Jan. 6, 2009).

[74]   Doe v. State, 111 A.3d 1077 (N.H. 2015) (registration requirements can only be applied to the petitioner if he is "promptly given an opportunity for either a court hearing, or an administrative hearing subject to judicial review, at which he is permitted to demonstrate that he no longer poses a risk sufficient to justify continued registration….[and] must be afforded periodic opportunities for further hearings, at reasonable intervals, to revisit whether registration continues to be necessary to protect the public").

[75]   Cappolino v. Commisioner, 102 A.3d 1254 (Pa. Commw. Ct. 2014). But see Commonwealth v. Perez, 97 A.3d 747 (Pa. Super. Ct. 2014) (retroactive application of new registration scheme did not violate the Ex Post Facto clause).

[76]   See, e.g., Doe v. Snyder, 932 F. Supp. 2d 803 (E.D. Mich. 2013) (addressing Michigan's 2011 amendments which substantially implemented SORNA); State v. Henry, 228 P.3d 900 (Ariz. Ct. App. 2010); Buffington v. State, 2008 Ark. LEXIS 71 (Jan. 31, 2008); Finnicum v. State, 673 S.E.2d 604 (Ga. 2009); State v. Yeoman, 236 P.3d 1265 (Idaho 2010); Illinois ex. rel. Birkett v. Konetski, 909 N.E.2d 783 (Ill. 2009); State v. Hunt, 2014 N.J. Super. Unpub. LEXIS 1424 (June 17, 2014); Smith v. Commonwealth, 743 S.E.2d 146 (Va. 2013); Kammerer v. State, 322 P.3d 827 (Wyo. 2014). In addition, one federal circuit has concluded that retroactive application of New York's registration amendments to an offender did not violate the Ex Post Facto clause. Doe v. Cuomo, 755 F.3d 105 (2d Cir. 2014).

[77]   Commonwealth v. Hainesworth, 82 A.3d 444 (Pa. 2014) (defendant entitled to specific performance of his plea agreement, a component of whose negotiation was that he would not be required to register as a sex offender). But see Commonwealth v. Giannatonio, 114 A.3d 429 (Pa. Super. Ct. 2015) (extension of state duration of registration period did not violate Ex Post Facto when conviction secured pursuant to federal plea agreement).

[78]   Doe v. Harris, 302 P.3d 598 (Cal. 2013).

[79]   ACLU v. Masto, 2:08-cv-00822-JCM-PAL (D. Nev., Oct. 7, 2008).

[80]   ACLU v. Masto, 670 F.3d 1046 (9th Cir. 2012). The Nevada Supreme Court also held that retroactive application of registration and notification requirements to juveniles adjudicated delinquent does not violate Due Process or the Ex Post Facto clause. State v. Eighth Jud. Dist. Ct., 306 P.3d 369 (Nev. 2013).

[81]   McCraw v. Gomez, 2014 Tex. App. LEXIS 13911 (1st Dist., Dec. 30, 2014).

[82]   State v. Jedlicka, 747 N.W.2d 580 (Minn. App. 2008); see also Flanders v. State, 955 N.E.2d 732 (Ind. App. 2011).

[83]   Buck v. Commonwealth, 308 S.W.3d 661 (Ky. 2010).

[84]   Moe v. Sex Offender Registry Board, 6 N.E.3d 530 (Mass. 2014).

[85]   See the procedure followed in Massachusetts, where the Sex Offender Registry Board must find that the offender poses a danger to the community before requiring registration: 803 CMR 106(B), available at http://www.mass.gov/eopss/docs/sorb/sor-regulations.pdf.

[86]   Doe v. Anderson, 108 A.3d 378 (Me. 2015) (holding, in part, that a guilty plea is not a 'criminal trial'). But see Bell v. Pennsylvania Board of Probation & Parole, 2014 Pa. Commw. Unpub. LEXIS 460 (July 24, 2014).

[87]   Doe v. Prosecutor, Marion County, 705 F.3d 694 (7th Cir. 2013) (statute prohibiting sex offenders from using social networking websites, instant messaging services, and chat programs violated the First Amendment); Doe v. State, 898 F.Supp.2d 1086 (D. Ne. 2012) (requirement to provide internet identifiers found unconstitutional on First Amendment and other grounds); Doe v. Shurtleff, 2008 U.S. Dist. LEXIS 73787 (D. Utah Sept. 25, 2008), vacated after legislative changes, 2009 U.S. Dist. LEXIS 73955 (D. Utah Aug. 20, 2009); Harris v. State, 985 N.E.2d 767 (Ind. Ct. App. 2013) (statute prohibiting use of a social networking site by a registered sex offender violated the First Amendment).

[88]   Brown v. Montoya, 662 F.3d 1152 (10th Cir. 2011).

[89]   State v. Briggs, 199 P.3d 935 (Utah 2008) ('target' information could include, among other things, a description of the offender's preferred victim demographics).

[90]   Ex parte Evans, 338 S.W.3d 545 (Tex. Crim. App. 2011).

[91]   Doe v. Jindal, 851 F. Supp.2d 995 (E.D. La. 2012).

[92]   Gonzalez v. Duncan, 551 F.3d 875 (9th Cir. 2008).

[93]   Bradshaw v. State, 671 S.E.2d 485 (Ga. 2008).

[94]   State v. Dipiazza, 778 N.W.2d 264 (Mich. Ct. App. 2009).

[95]   Doe v. Keathley, 2009 Mo. App. LEXIS 4 (Jan. 6, 2009). But see State v. Hough, 978 N.E.2d 505 (Ind. Ct. App. 2012); Andrews v. State, 978 N.E.2d 494 (Ind. Ct. App. 2012) (states without deciding that the federal duty to register could apply if the offender engaged in interstate travel).

[96]   In re McClain, 741 S.E.2d 893 (N.C. 2013) (North Carolina's registration law directly incorporates the clean record provisions of SORNA); see In re Hall, 768 S.E.2d 39 (N.C. Ct. App. 2014) (using SORNA's tiering structure).

[97]   State v. Nieman, 84 A.2d 603 (Pa. 2013).

[98]   530 U.S. 466 (2000).

[99]   See People v. Mosley, 344 P.3d 788 (Cal. 2015) (residency restrictions are not 'punishment' for the purposes of Sixth Amendment analysis); Colorado v. Rowland, 207 P.3d 890 (Colo. Ct. App. 2009); State v. Meredith, 2008 Minn. App. Unpub. LEXIS 324 (April 8, 2008).

[100]   The American Bar Association's Collateral Consequences Project, http://www.abacollateralconsequences.org, has produced a standing resource which lists all collateral consequences which flow at the federal and state level for convictions of certain crimes. Users may select 'sex offenses' as a search term and view all of the collateral consequences which may be imposed on persons so convicted.

[101]   See United States v. Cottle, 355 Fed. Appx. 18 (6th Cir. 2009); Mireles v. Bell, 2008 U.S. Dist. LEXIS 2451 (D. Mich. Jan. 11, 2008); State v. Flowers, 249 P.3d 367 (Idaho 2011); Magyar v. State, 18 So.3d 807 (Miss. 2009) (citing thorough collection of controlling case law across the country); People v. Gravino, 928 N.E.2d 1048 (N.Y. 2010) (guilty plea); State v. Nash, 48 A.D.3d 837 (N.Y. App. Div. 3d Dep't 2008); see also United States v. Molina, 68 M.J. 532 (U.S.C.G. CCA 2009) (mutual misunderstanding of registration requirement was grounds for withdrawing a guilty plea entered pursuant to

a plea agreement); State v. Bowles, 89 A.D.3d 171 (N.Y. App. Div. 2011) (offender has the right to the effective assistance of counsel in a risk level assessment (SORA) hearing).

[102]   U.S. v. Riley, 72 M.J. 115 (C.A.A.F. 2013) (substantial basis to question the providence of guilty plea when the judge failed to ensure that the defendant understood the registration requirements associated with a plea of guilty). The Riley decision was clarified in U.S. v. Talkington, 73 M.J. 212 (2014) as applying only to considerations raised by the Padilla case and its progeny regarding the voluntariness of guilty pleas, and is further clarified in Washington v. U.S., 74 M.J. 560 (A.C.C.A. 2014), as not applying retroactively.

[103]   United States v. Rose, 2010 CCA LEXIS 251 (A.F. Ct. Crim. App. June 11, 2010). Contra Edmonds v. Pruett, 2014 U.S. Dist. LEXIS 116736 (E.D. Va. Aug. 20, 2014).

[104]   People v. Fonville, 804 N.W.2d 878 (Mich. Ct. App. 2011).

[105]   559 U.S. 356 (2010).

[106]

[107]   Rodriguez-Moreno v. Oregon, 2011 U.S. Dist. LEXIS 151123 (D. Or. Nov. 15, 2011) (failure to advise of registration requirements is not ineffective assistance of counsel); Illinois v. Cowart, 28 N.E.3d 862 (Ill. App. 2015) (trial court failure to admonish regarding registration requirements is not constitutionally deficient). Contra Taylor v. State, 698 S.E.2d 384 (Ga. Ct. App. 2010); People v. Dodds, 7 N.E.3d 83 (Ill. Ct. App. 2014); People v. Fonville, 804 N.W.2d 878 (Mich. Ct. App. 2011); State v. Trammell, 336 P.3d 977 (2014) (N.M. Ct. App. 2014); State v. Trotter, 2014 Utah LEXIS 72 (May 20, 2014).

[108]   Chaidez v. U.S., 133 S.Ct. 1103 (2013).

[109]   132 S.Ct. 2566 (2012).

[110]   133 S.Ct. 1863 (2013).

[111]   See U.S. v. Anderson, 771 F.3d 1064 (8th Cir. 2014); U.S. v. Robbins, 729 F.3d 131 (2d Cir. 2013) (unsuccessful argument that an interstate travel prosecution under 18 U.S.C. § 2250 was precluded by the decision in Sebelius, i.e., that the government cannot prosecute 'inactivity'); U.S. v. Piper, 2013 U.S. Dist. LEXIS 113059 (D. Vt. Aug. 12, 2013) (successful argument under Chevron that the SORNA Final Guidelines must be followed in determining whether someone is required to register under SORNA).

[112]   Smith v. Commonwealth, 743 S.E.2d 146 (Va. 2013).

[113]   State v. Larson, 2008 Minn. App. Unpub. LEXIS 1525 (Dec. 30, 2008); State v. Sparks, 657 S.E.2d 655 (N.C. 2008); State v. Green, 230 P.3d 654 (Wash. App. 2010).

[114]   Meza v. Livingston, 607 F.3d 392 (5th Cir. 2010) (defendant had a liberty interest in being free from registration requirements where he had not been convicted of a sex offense); State v. Arthur H., 953 A.2d 630 (Conn. 2008) (no due process hearing required); Doe v. Dep't of Public Safety, 971 A.2d 975 (Md. App. 2009) (presumption of dangerousness flowing from a rape conviction was permissible); Smith v. Commonwealth, 743 S.E.2d 146 (Va. 2013).

[115]   Litmon v. Harris, 768 F.3d 1237 (9th Cir 2014) (requiring sexually violent predators to check in every 90 days did not violate substantive due process); Woe v. Spitzer, 571 F.Supp.2d 382 (E.D. N.Y. 2008) (when amended statute extended the registration period by ten years three days before petitioner's registration requirement expired, there was no protected liberty interest).

[116]   Doe v. Jindal, 2011 U.S. Dist. LEXIS 100408 (E.D. La., Sept. 7, 2011); State v. Dickerson, 97 A.3d 15 (Conn. App. 2014). California has a long line of cases litigating equal protection issues in sex offender registration cases, based on People v. Hofsheier, 129 P.3d 29 (Cal. 2006), which was recently overruled in Johnson v. Cal. Dep't of Justice, 341 P.3d 1075 (Cal. 2015).

[117]   See Thomas v. United States, 942 A.2d 1180 (D.C. 2008) (underlying misdemeanor charges which required registration upon conviction were "petty" for purposes of the Sixth Amendment, and a jury trial was not required); In re Richard A., 946 A.2d 204 (R.I. 2008). But see Fushek v. State, 183 P.3d 536 (Ariz. 2008) (because of the seriousness of the consequences of being designated a sex offender, jury trial must be afforded when there is a special allegation of sexual motivation in a misdemeanor case).

[118]   Washington v. Smith, 344 P.3d 1244 (Wash. App. 2015).

[119]   People v. Nichols, 176 Cal. App. 4th 428 (3d Dist. 2009) (28 years to life sentence for failure to register under California's three-strikes law did not violate the 8th Amendment); People v. T.D., 823

N.W.2d 101 (Mich. 2011) (requiring a juvenile to register was not cruel and unusual punishment), dismissed as moot, 821 N.W.2d 569 (Mich. 2012).

[120] Rosin v. Monken, 599 F.3d 574 (7th Cir. 2010) (an offender convicted in New York was promised in his plea agreement that he would never have to register as a sex offender, but when he moved to Illinois and was required to register under its laws, it was not a violation of the Full Faith and Credit Clause); see Burton v. State, 977 N.E.2d 1004 (Ind. Ct. App. 2012) (State unsuccessfully argued that the Full Faith and Credit clause should apply).

[121] United States v. King, 431 Fed. Appx. 630 (10th Cir. 2011).

[122] State v. Caton, 260 P.3d 946 (Wash. Ct. App. 2011), rev'd on other grounds, 273 P.3d 980 (Wash. 2012).

[123] Proponents of the sovereign citizen movement "believe they are not subject to federal or state statutes or proceedings, reject most forms of taxation as illegitimate, and place special significance on commercial law." U.S. v. Harding, 2013 U.S. Dist. LEXIS 62471 (W.D. Va., May 1, 2013) (18 U.S.C. §2250 prosecution), quoting U.S. v. Brown, 669 F.3d 10 (1st Cir. 2012). In Harding the defendant argued that the federal court did not have jurisdiction over him, citing the Organic Act of 1871, the fact that his name was listed in all caps on the indictment, that there was no corpus delicti for the offense, and that the federal court was an 'Admiralty Court' because the flag in the courtroom had fringe on it. Id. at *3-*15.

[124] 131 S.Ct. 2355 (2011), on remand at 681 F.3d 149 (3d Cir. 2012), cert. granted. on other grounds, 133 S.Ct. 978 (2013). Thus far, Tenth Amendment challenges raised under Bond have been unsuccessful. See U.S. v. Kidd, 2013 U.S. App. LEXIS 5032 (6th Cir., Mar. 11, 2013); U.S. v. Smith, 504 Fed. Appx. 519 (8th Cir. 2012).

[125] See United States v. Reynolds, 132 S.Ct. 975 (2012).

[126] See United States v. Ogburn, 590 Fed. Appx. 683 (9th Cir. 2015); State v. Cook, 187 P.3d 1283 (Kan. 2008); Longoria v. State, 749 N.W.2d 104 (Minn. App. 2008).

[127] In re C.P.W., 213 P.3d 413 (Kan. 2009); People v. Haddock, 852 N.Y.S.2d 441 (N.Y. App. Div. 2008); State v. Vick, 2010 Wash. App. LEXIS 2462 (Nov. 2, 2010).

[128] Christie v. State, 2008 Ark. App. LEXIS 10 (Jan. 9, 2008); State v. T.R.D., 942 A.2d 1000 (Conn. 2008).

[129] Petway v. State, 661 S.E.2d 667 (Ga. App. 2008) (pre-release notice of registration requirements is not a prerequisite to the obligation to register); Barrientos v. State, 2013 Tex. App. LEXIS 7712 (June 24, 2013) (primarily Spanish-speaking defendant properly convicted even when all notices were in English and he claimed he did not understand his responsibilities).

[130] See United States v. Leach, 2009 U.S. Dist. LEXIS 104703 (D. Ind. Nov. 6, 2009); United States v. Benevento, 633 F. Supp. 2d 1170 (D. Nev. 2009); State v. Bryant, 614 S.E.2d 479, 488 (N.C. 2005) ("the pervasiveness of sex offender registration programs [combined with additional factors in this case] certainly constitute circumstances which would lead the reasonable individual to inquire of a duty to register in any state upon relocation").

[131] State v. Binnarr, 733 S.E.2d 890 (S.C. 2012) (notice of changed registration responsibilities sought to be proven by way of an unreturned letter, without more, does not prove actual notice sufficient to prosecute for failure to register).

[132] State v. White, 58 A.3d 643 (N.H. 2012) (defendant failed to report the creation of a MySpace account).

[133] State v. Lee, 286 P.3d 537 (Idaho 2012).

[134] State v. Peterson, 186 P.3d 1179 (Wash. App. 2008).

[135] See, e.g., Cal. Penal Code §3003.5 (2012); Idaho Code § 18-8329 (2012); 57 Okla. Stat. (2012). §590

[136] In re William Taylor, 343 P.3d 867 (Cal. 2015).

[137] G.H. v. Twp. of Galloway, 951 A.2d 221 (N.J. 2008) (New Jersey law preempted municipal residency restrictions); People v. Diack, 26 N.E.3d 1151 (N.Y. 2015) (New York law preempts local residency restriction provisions); People v. Oberlander, 880 N.Y.S.2d 875 (N.Y. Sup. Ct. 2009) (Rockland County residency restriction preempted by New York state law); People v. Blair, 873 N.Y.S.2d 890 (Albany City Ct. 2009) (Albany County residency restriction preempted by New York state law). Contra

United States v. King, 2009 U.S. Dist. LEXIS 94582 (W.D. Okla. Oct. 9, 2009) (Oklahoma's residency restrictions did not present an obstacle to complying with federal sex offender registration requirements).

[138] See Commonwealth v. Baker, 295 S.W.3d 437 (Ky. 2009) (Kentucky's residency restrictions exceeded the nonpunitive purpose of public safety and thus violated the Ex Post Facto clause); see also Duarte v. City of Lewisville, 759 F.3d 514 (5th Cir. 2014) (standing granted in challenge to residence restrictions suit). But see McAteer v. Riley, 2008 U.S. Dist. LEXIS 26209 (M.D. Ala. March 31, 2008) ("The court expresses no opinion today on whether McAteer could present evidence and arguments to establish by the clearest proof that the residency and employment restrictions violate the Ex Post Facto clause and leaves that question for another day").

[139] State v. Stark, 802 N.W.2d 165 (S.D. 2011) (discussing state-level loitering and safety zone provisions).

[140] http://www.smart.gov/pdfs/MTSOR_Code.pdf.

[141] For example, the Confederated Tribes of the Umatilla Indian Reservation (CTUIR) was one of the first tribes to implement SORNA, and met all of SORNA's requirements in doing so, see the SMART Office's Substantial Implementation Report at http://www.smart.gov/pdfs/sorna/ ConfTribes- UmatillaIndianReservation.pdf. CTUIR is located entirely within the State of Oregon, which falls short of many of SORNA's provisions. Maxine Bernstein, Sex Offenders in Oregon: State Fails to Track Hundreds, THE OREGONIAN (Oct. 2, 2013), available at http://www.oregonlive.com/ sexoffenders/special- presentation/ (Oregon only posts 2.5% of its registered sex offenders on its public sex offender registry website).

[142] See United States v. Nichols, 2014 U.S. Dist. LEXIS 118129 (D. S.D., Aug. 20, 2014) (tribes have the inherent power to exclude outsiders from their territory).

[143] Kirkaldie v. United States, 2014 U.S. Dist. LEXIS 72041 (D. Mont. May 22, 2014) (domestic violence prosecution); United States v. First, 731 F.3d 998 (9th Cir. 2013) (admissible so long as the uncounseled conviction would not violate the U.S. Constitution) (possession of a firearm prosecution); United States v. Shavanaux, 647 F.3d 993 (11th Cir. 2011) (tribal court convictions that meet the due process requirements of the Indian Civil Rights Act (ICRA) may be admitted in subsequent federal prosecutions) (domestic violence prosecution); United States v. Cavanaugh, 643 F.3d 592 (8th Cir. 2011) (domestic violence prosecution). But see United States v. Bryant, 769 F.3d 671 (9th Cir. 2014) (tribal court convictions for domestic violence, obtained without any right to counsel, may not be used in recidivist prosecution). There are also cases that have interpreted the above decisions, see, e.g., United States v. Bundy, 966 F.Supp. 2d 1175 (D. N.M. 2013) (tribal conviction did not meet the Shavanaux test) (DUI prosecution).

[144] State v. Atcitty, 215 P.3d 90 (N.M. 2009).

[145] United States v. Begay, 622 F.3d 1187 (9th Cir. 2010), abrogated on other grounds, United States v. DeJarnette, 741 F.3d 971 (9th Cir. 2013).

[146] State v. John, 308 P.3d 1208 (Ct. App. Ariz. 2013).

[147] Supplemental Guidelines, supra note 7 at 1637-38.

[148] United States v. Nichols, 775 F.3d 1225 (10th Cir. 2014); United States. v. Forster, 549 Fed. Appx. 757 (10th Cir. 2013); United States v. Murphy, 664 F.3d 798 (10th Cir. 2011); Carr v. United States, 2014 U.S. Dist. LEXIS 21262 (M.D. Tenn., Feb. 20, 2014); United States v. Nichols, 2013 U.S. Dist. LEXIS 160804) (D. Kan. Nov. 12, 2013).

[149] U.S. v. Lunsford, 725 F.3d 859 (8th Cir. 2013); Ward v. U.S., 2014 U.S. Dist. LEXIS 160392 (N.D. Fla., Nov. 14, 2014).

[150] The Canadian Province of Alberta maintains a website listing high-risk sex offenders: www.solgps.alberta.ca/SAFE_COMMUNITIES/COMMUNITY_AWARENESS/SERIOUS_VIOLENT_O FFENDERS/Pages/default.aspx, and Saskatchewan maintains a listing of certain high-risk offenders which includes information about certain sex offenders: http://www.justice.gov.sk.ca/PN-List. South Korea, http://www.sexoffender.go kr, and the Province of Western Australia, https://www.communityprotection.wa.gov.au, also have public websites where information about sex offenders is posted.

[151] There is a disclosure scheme in place in the United Kingdom authorizing law enforcement to provide details of certain sex offenders, http://www homeoffice.gov.uk/crime/child-sex-offender- disclosure.

[152] Available at http://www.smart.gov/pdfs/GlobalOverview.pdf. In 2013, GAO did a full review of the Registered Sex Offender International Tracking System which is in development by a working group spearheaded by the SMART Office. GAO-13-200, REGISTERED SEX OFFENDERS: SHARING MORE INFORMATION WILL ENABLE FEDERAL AGENCIES TO IMPROVE NOTIFICATIONS OF SEX OFFENDERS' INTERNATIONAL TRAVEL (2013), available at http://www.gao.gov/assets/660/652194.pdf.

[153] The fact that a person has been convicted of a sex offense involving children can result in the revocation of a person's Ham radio license. FCC Reverses ALJ's Decision, Revokes Convicted Sex Offender's Ham License, ARRL.ORG, http://www.arrl.org/news/fcc-reverses-alj-s-decision-revokes-convicted-sex-offender-s-amateur-radio-license (Nov. 13, 2014). In at least one state, there is a statutory presumption against any registered sex offender being granted unsupervised visitation, custody, or residential placement of a child. 13 DEL. CODE ANN. §724A.

[154] See BLACK'S LAW DICTIONARY (Abr. 6th ed., 1991) at p. 288.

[155] Balentine v. Tremblay, 554 Fed. Appx. 58 (2d Cir. 2014).

[156] Bushra v. Holder, 529 Fed. Appx. 659 (6th Cir. 2013) (conviction for failure to register is a crime involving moral turpitude). Contra Mohamed v. Holder, 769 F.3d 885 (4th Cir. 2014); Efange v. Holder, 642 F.3d 918 (10th Cir. 2011); Plascencia-Ayala v. Mukasey, 516 F.3d 738 (9th Cir. 2008), overruled on other grounds by Marmolejo-Campos v. Holder, 558 F.3d 903 (9th Cir. 2009).

[157] Meyer v. Nat'l Tenant Network, Inc., 2014 U.S. Dist. LEXIS 6797 (N.D. Cal., Jan. 17, 2014).

[158] Santos v. State, 668 S.E.2d 676 (Ga. 2008) (registration requirements unconstitutionally vague); Rodriguez v. Maryland, 108 A.3d 438 (Md. Ct. App. 2015) (weekly registration requirement for homeless offenders not unconstitutional); State v. Crofton, 2008 Wash. App. LEXIS 1283 (June 2, 2008) (weekly registration requirement for homeless offenders permissible).

[159] See Saiger v. City of Chicago, 2014 U.S. Dist. LEXIS 83206 (N.D. Ill., June 19, 2014) (permitting plaintiff's Due Process claim to proceed); Derfus v. City of Chicago, 2014 U.S. Dist. LEXIS 68844 (N.D. Ill. May 20, 2014); Beley v. City of Chicago, 2013 U.S. Dist. LEXIS 90070 (N.D. Ill., June 27, 2013); People v. Wlecke, 6 N.E.3d 745 (Ill. Ct. App. 2014) (offender who lacked identification and was turned away from registering could not be convicted for failure to register).

[160] See People v. Deluca, 176 Cal. Rptr. 3d 419 (Cal. App. 2d Dist. 2014) (even though shelter had limited hours, it counted as a 'residence' for the purposes of registration); State v. Allman, 321 P.3d 557 (Co. Ct. App. 2012) (offender used his car as a residence when working away from 'home' during the week, was a 'residence' for purposes of the statute); Branch v. State, 917 N.E.2d 1283 (Ind. Ct. App. 2009) (homeless defendant was successfully prosecuted for failure to register when he failed to inform authorities that he had left a shelter); Milliner v. State, 890 N.E.2d 789 (Ind. Ct. App. 2008) (offender kicked out of house by wife and staying with friends had to update his registration every time he moved); Tobar v. State, 284 S.W.3d 133 (Ky. 2009) (when offender did not notify authorities of leaving homeless shelter, conviction for failure to register was proper); State v. Samples, 198 P.3d 803 (Mont. 2008) (when offender failed to notify authorities of leaving shelter, conviction was proper); Commonwealth v. Wilgus, 40 A.3d 1201 (Pa. Super. 2009) (where defendant was unable to rent a room at his intended residence he had a duty to inform registry officials of a change of address); Breeden v. State, 2008 Tex. App. LEXIS 2150 (March 26, 2008) (offender who moved out of hotel into car in parking lot of hotel properly convicted and sentenced to 55 years). But see Commonwealth v. Bolling, 893 N.E.2d 371 (Mass. App. 2008) (offender did not need to update his address when he found a friend willing to take him in for a few days); State v. Dinkins, 339 Wis.2d 78 (2012) (offender was charged with failure to register, prior to release from incarceration, for failure to provide a residence address, and this was not permissible).

[161] Lamberty v. Delaware, 108 A.3d 1225 (Del. 2015).

[162] United States v. Pendleton, 2009 U.S. Dist. LEXIS 85347 (D. Del. Sept. 18, 2009).

[163] State v. Edwards, 87 A.3d 1144 (Conn. Ct. App. 2014).

[164] Nikolaev v. State, 2014 Tex. App. LEXIS 2246 (Tex. Ct. App., Feb. 27, 2014).

[165] 42 U.S.C. § 13663; see also Denial of Admission and Termination of Assistance for Criminals and Alcohol Abusers, 24 C.F.R. 982.553(a)(2) (2015); When Must I Prohibit Admission of Sex Offenders?, 24

C.F.R. §5.856 (2001); To What Criminal Records and Searches Does this Subpart Apply?, 24 C.F.R. §5.901 (2001); What Special Authority is there to Obtain Access to Sex Offender Registration Information?, 24 C.F.R. §5.905 (2001), 24 C.F.R. 960.204(a)(4); Denial of Admission for Criminal Activity or Drug Abuse by Household Members (2001). HUD issued guidance in 2012 describing the duties of owners, agents, and public housing authorities with regards to admitting registered sex offenders. State Registered Lifetime Sex Offenders in Federally Assisted Housing, http://portal.hud.gov/hudportal/documents/huddoc?id=12-28pihn12-11hsgn.pdf. This guidance was drafted in part as a response to an Inspector General's report which had been issued in 2009. HUD SUBSIDIZED AN ESTIMATED 2,094 TO 3,046 HOUSEHOLDS THAT INCLUDED LIFETIME REGISTERED SEX OFFENDERS, AUDIT REP'T NO. 2009-KC-0001 (Aug. 14, 2009), https://www.hudoig.gov/sites/default/files/pdf/Internal/2009/ig0970001.pdf.

[166] 'Section 8' is the common shorthand reference to the housing assistance provisions contained in the United States Housing Act of 1937, ch. 896, Title I, § 8 (Sept. 1, 1937), as amended.

[167] Miller v. McCormick, 605 F.Supp.2d 296 (D. Me. 2009).

[168] Johnson v. California, 2011 U.S. Dist. LEXIS 101623 (C.D. Cal. July 25, 2011).

[169] Henley v. Housing Auth. of New Orleans, 2013 U.S. Dist. LEXIS 62255 (E.D. La. May 1, 2013).

[170] Tristan v. State, 393 S.W. 3d 806 (Ct. App. Tex. 2012). Contra Dingman v. Cart Shield USA, LLC, 2013 U.S. Dist. LEXIS 93551 (S.D. Fla., July 3, 2013) (failure to register not proven to involve a dishonest act or false statement).

[171] Statute addressed in U.S. v. Walizer, 600 Fed. Appx. 546 (9th Cir. 2015). In Alleyne v. United States, 133 S.Ct. 2151 (2013), the Supreme Court concluded that "any fact that increases the mandatory minimum is an 'element' that must be submitted to the jury." Id.

[172] U.S. v. Hardeman, 704 F.3d 1266 (9th Cir. 2013).

www.ingramcontent.com/pod-product-compliance
Lightning Source LLC
Chambersburg PA
CBHW081315180526
45170CB00007B/2711

* 9 781541 202764 *